RIPPLE EFFECT

GW00801916

for Joanna

RIPPLE EFFECT

Terry McDonagh

ARLEN
HOUSE

Ripple Effect

is published in 2013 by
ARLEN HOUSE
42 Grange Abbey Road
Baldoyle
Dublin 13
Ireland
Phone/Fax: 353 86 8207617
Email: arlenhouse@gmail.com

Distributed internationally by
SYRACUSE UNIVERSITY PRESS
621 Skytop Road, Suite 110
Syracuse, NY 13244–5290
Phone: 315–443–5534/Fax: 315–443–5545
Email: supress@syr.edu

ISBN 978–1–85132–062–2, paperback

Typesetting: Arlen House
Printing: Brunswick Press
Cover Images: Sally McKenna
Front Cover Image: 'The Equinox, Lough Crew Cairn T'
watercolour and ink, 15" by 21"
Back Cover Image: Medicine Wheel, acrylic on canvas
stretched on a twisted willow hoop, 3.5 foot circle
www.sallymckenna.com

CONTENTS

ACKNOWLEDGEMENTS

Thanks to the editors of the following publications: *The SHOp; Agenda Poetry; Poetry Ireland Review; Revival Journal; The Stony Thursday Book; Prairie Schooner; The Fish Anthology*. Midwest Radio.

'Journey of a Pebble' was commissioned by Elizabeth McKenzie, Tinteán, Melbourne.

'In the End ...' was commissioned by Tuam Cancer Care.

RIPPLE EFFECT

RIPPLE EFFECT

When you throw a stone
into a pond
you can't predict the ripples,
for so much depends on
the cut of the stone,
the way you throw it,
the water and the wind.

HERE COMES PARADISE ...

Caesar conquered France, but no man's been able
to make an impression on this country-lane goddess,

who tosses her head at exhibitions with an ex, ogles
out of *orse 'n ound* gossip pages or splashes herself

the length of her stride in an encore way of walking.
One punter pledges to polish her bike and blush like

a jockey under streetlamps. Ministers woo with silk,
pearls and handcuffs, while rugby-types try wrestling,

or cat-calls in forests and hazel woods. And this little
cherry bud will say: *leave love out of this. I'll share*

a fragrant hour – a fling with you – thrills of the body,
but my heart can't keep pace with the speed of my retreat.

She is a disco queen, a flirt on moss – a full stop. She's
pearl of the morning and sunray of the evening, but if

a man dares to bathe in the warm wind of this creature,
he has himself to blame when she stuffs him into

the back seat of his Mini, has her vile way with him,
steps out, slams his door, rights her tights and rambles off.

No man's been able to take her breath away: not a Brit
in codpiece – not an Irish hijacker on a sly landscape ...

there goes Paradise.

Rundown Town

Nobody cared about the priest
in Rundown Town,
not even when he whispered *help*
through his porous front door,
so he got fed up and pedalled
the hundred miles or so to the city.
Shabby enough to be a poet,
he gulped long drinks and settled
great questions by reiterating:
the road is an end in itself and
no one travels without purpose.

Some critics were confused, but
helped him into bed with Pinkie,
who hated curtains – but got him
his first bursary.
She took to women and he became
the prophet of a dark place
– men were mentioned.
In one interview, he insisted
he was never far from a bullfight,
a battered bike or poker game,
and he adored brown bread.

Time did what it does to priests,
cats, poets, bats and bankers, and
with his final wish – to be borne
the hundred miles or so
to Rundown Cemetery – granted,
he gulped a final glass
and passed on, smiling.
His funeral was the largest
ever seen in Rundown Town.

It hadn't snowed for days and what remained
was discoloured by grit and dog piss –

a bar on a busy corner was blue with
temptation and tomfoolery. It was *Silvester*.

Ernst tripped up the third step of three,
but saved face. This was his church.

He went for a stool along the counter,
ordered a Merlot, then checked patrons

in the mirror behind the optics.
Wine replaced his need for words.

The sculpture of a woman – a Christmas tree
blazing at her feet – came into focus on

the back wall. No trace of Father Christmas.
He tried to remember his father, but that was

when he was three. A Moulin Rouge poster
filled a space on the wall. The sculpture

seemed to have a sword between her shoulders.
Her breasts were bare. *Another wine?*

In the lurid air, the figure could have been
foreign – a mother, perhaps. A fly, unable

to get its wings going, crawled by his glass
like an ageing actor with walk-on, walk-off parts.

Ernst felt for the slim volume in his inside pocket.
It was louder outside – he'd have to mind his step.

THEIR SECRET

Loud music ... late ... young people – hardly
the place for established couples discussing

the futility of a son's dream to embark on
a literary career at twenty-eight. I was

eavesdropping: the son had a partner, a baby
in waiting, a bike and no visible means of income,

but had they looked around them, they'd
have seen carbon copies of that son, and if

they'd cast their minds back thirty years,
they have seen themselves sidestepping punk

for easy dance-floor music, and hairstyles with
rotary club cards and television tokens attached.

They have nothing to fear: they have alarms,
word-of-the-day cars and children that do

the right thing in the end – *but why this pub*
is the secret they are not prepared to share.

FOX AMONG THE FANS

Fox has been going to home games for years.
He's aged, but his coat has held its colour.
No barking or yowling at stars these days – just
a wave, wink, good to be alive without ambush or trap.

Fox was candid on a late night talk show: chicks
had been cautious about his advances *with some*
justification, he conceded, but he'd never touch a nugget,
not even if – never! It was free-range or nothing.

He recounted being set upon by a party of dogs
and rescued by animal lovers who'd given him a home
and season ticket. The media adored his tweets on
old-style scarecrows in tasteless hats and noses.

When asked why he rarely missed a game, he said
he enjoyed meeting friend Reynard with leash, and
watching Redhead, a striker of instinct and stealth
– *must be some fox in his gene pool*. Wild applause.

And on one occasion, as the sun burst on to the pitch,
he dreamt he was in a cluster of stars: *could I be a fox*
among the fairies? Encore. *More.* He smiled, admitted
being happy that his coat had held its colour, but when

he'd scented the haunting fur of an old vixen flame
draped across a fat person's back, he shed a tear, for he
remembered sharing a limb or two with her in a meadow.

Pre-chicken-battery days had been more graceful:
winters were hard, but there'd been open seasons
with fair game to look forward to in those shoeless days,

but spare me a thought: my hunting days are
done and I am perched and stuffed behind plastic
like a bishop in muse costume on a high altar.

While bombs were falling on Asian soil,
the puppet class was called upon to down tools
and listen to the President's master plan
in case of a bomb threat:
We will run to an open field.
You will be safe in that field.
It is a model battlefield, he assured them.
There are flags everywhere.
He had his directives from on high, he said.

One bemused girl asked if they could wear masks
as a form of protection. The President said:
Yes, a novel idea.
There could be blackened faces like brave soldiers
and gas masks in case of fallout.
They all giggled. He didn't.
War is a serious business. It will always be with us.

A senior student suggested they read poetry
and sang in the open field – and it might rain.
The President clicked his heels and said
there would be no talking, noise or absurdities
in public – in particular on fields of battle
and, as a senior student, she should know
that poetry and singing belonged to choirs and
classrooms:
if you want to be silly later in life,
you can join a theatre company.

They were now at school learning the hard facts.
When the war was over, visual arts students
would be working on a monument to an unknown soldier
and young poets could write laments to their dead heroes.

One student took a puppet out of his pocket
and held it up for all to see.

And what is that, young man?
It's a puppet, Sir.
It looks like a soldier.
It is a soldier, Sir.

The President scratched his head. He was happy to say
there would be an information screen with
honours lists and military updates along the hedgerows.

A small boy made his way to the front, raised his hand
and politely asked where the field was. The President
looked confused, but reassured the boy it was on its way
and it would do us proud.

All but one of the class took out their puppets.

TREE MUSIC

There's a young beech
in the heart
of our wild garden
and this morning as
summer sun pierced
the thick outer hedge
to light up the tree,
you just knew there
was a god of a kind
and when a light breeze
joined in
I couldn't choose to hear
or not to hear.

POLICE AND DONKEY IN A HIT AND RUN
April 2012

Last week, at the AGM of the Irish State Police,
concern about the cost of transport was expressed.

Of the twenty-five million at their disposal,
eleven-and-a-half went towards repairs.

In one case, in a late-night hit and run involving
a police car and a donkey, the cost of repairs

was more than the car was worth and, as there
was no question of police culpability or mention

of the animal, we can assume it was either dead,
had escaped with minor injuries, or had legged it

without trace – in which case the police, countrywide,
would be alerted and no money or manpower spared

in satisfying the courts that everything in police power
had been done to show the donkey up in a bad light.

THE SINGER

It wasn't so much the song
as the person
and you couldn't say
it was the person either.

Perhaps it was the ring
of the day
that made her sing.

BODY LANGUAGE

Between showers at a bus stop in Hamburg,
a story dropped *ping* into my lap:

a handbag, about as big as a book,
pitched from a bike near a roundabout.
A taxi avoided the bag.
Stopped.
Traffic struggled like an aggravated eel.

The taxi man and woman-bike-owner
examined the bag in mime sketches,
then sidled off silent as snow – never once

looking each other in the eye
or raising an eyebrow?

I tried to interpret the language
of their meeting
but it skulked and floated off like a funeral.

Perhaps songbirds can translate
from their branches of light
that hang between the beads of rain.

A story fell *ping* into my lap as birds
continued singing for me
and for people I didn't grow up with.

ADIEU

After years of hard tackling,
goal-getting, miss-kicking,

and having learned everything
about life, the player took

a length of cord and went
down to the dark corner

behind the garden shed
to hang up his boots.

I DREAM OF BEING YOUR DICTATOR
ON A COUNTY COUNCIL TICKET
for a certain politician who attends funerals

I'm your man. I made the map, drew
all the boundaries, paid for lamp-posts,
cut down forests, wrote statutory laws,
and saw to it that town limits
were protected by walls and spotlights.

I see myself in a minefield with helmet,
gun and flag warning of the dangers
of open spaces and flying objects.

Things are not tidy. People will have to
fight again. I enjoy polishing big gates
and beheadings. I am nearly everywhere.

I am in charge of your dreams.
I never miss a funeral.

As a would-be imperialist, I repeat plots
to myself in happy rooms. I have paid

for high fences round schools,
encouraged lawn-cutting,
supported sensible priests,
censored and streamlined books,
banished foreign influences,
set up institutions for the left-handed
and therapies for the weak at mathematics
– best of all
I've devised a shrink-kit for liberal know-alls.

Here at the edge of my district,
I see lots of unfinished work:

three untagged frogs,
one set of weeds,
a youth out of uniform,
an artist without permit,
a bundle of wild flowers,
a man without a tie,
an untrimmed hedge,
an unregistered bird's nest,
a non-baptised child,
a cluster of unruly heather,
a live hare,
wasters by the wayside,
a poster for poetry.

Things are not tidy. People will
have to fight again. I enjoy
financing big gates and beheadings.
I am nearly everywhere.

I am your dream tyrant.
I never miss a funeral.

I used to order keepers of the peace
to have the last citizen under curfew
as darkness settled between houses.

I've always had the support of
sturdy cardinals,
tycoon builders,
strict teachers,
corpulent law makers,
state scientists,
huge farmers,
but never of humanitarian dicks,
never of the young and selfish.

I used professional help
to have them farmed out
to harder work in wilder places.

Years ago, a self-styled philosopher began
to spread words and propaganda about
the need to concentrate on liberty and death.

I gave him all the death he'd ever dreamed of
and I pushed the graveyard out of town
to keep the memory of his bones from our youth.

I am your philosophy.
I never miss a funeral.

No matter how much you poison weeds,
they come back.

I govern from a high window.
Let the souls of the dead

fly around hedgerows and chimney pots
if that's their innermost wish.

My monuments are built.
Let history-makers sit in their hilltop tents.

I am your dream man on the Council.
I'll always show up. Believe me.

There we were: arm-in-arm,
halfway along Church Road,
just past the graveyard
and Unadopted Highway
on our way to stock up on
Crow's Landing – a Californian Savignon

when you pointed to a window
like someone in touch with an oracle.
I looked to your feet to see if scales
had fallen from your eyes and listened
for a song, but all you said was *parrot*.

The street had become a mountainside;
the drapes an entrance to a grotto
with a huge pink parrot perched
in a floor-to-ceiling cage. It slept.
We stood. We gaped.
A child muse snapped the drapes shut.

Wow! What was that? I turned
to look down at my own shoes.
Dunno … wonder what it feeds on?
A diet of forbidden fruit, I bet.
A god must be in the thick of it.

Now back to breath and speech, we went
for happy wine, then sidled back
past the house and graveyard like laughing cats
as the streets retreated into the sunset.
In the morning we noticed the first daffodils.
Pinkish balloons on the hedge
swayed like mind-trappers,
like misunderstood symbols – like dissolving music.

A Singer in a Mythical City

I often hear voices in my sleep,
little mystical things
mutating and staying small, like

random episodes so silent
that I never know whether
it's singing for its own sake,

someone pleading to be saved
from out of their depth, or
disjointed words in the breeze.

I'm trying to talk about language
here – to talk-time as a film,
without image to support meaning.

I challenge metaphor to take control
of destiny as Oskar did
in Günter Grass's *Blechtrommel*.

I have five senses to breathe in
and out: to taste money; to hear
the fat of men on shoreline tankers;

to smell no end to lines of children
waiting to be transported past rows
of scented flowers to certain death.

I could try to taste the terror of height
when your tower is lost on the Atlantic
and I am the singer in a mythical city.

I am touched by my life overseas,
dining with icons, talking for tea,
trying to recall an elusive address.

THE LAST BARD
for Sally McKenna, creator of the Raftery sculpture, Kiltimagh

On *Lios Árd* among beech trees, I lie
like a novice on moss and grass and
you are in those battered clouds
looking down at colours you know by heart.

I was a fierce warrior here at eight.
At nine, I hacked my name into a tree.
A dog howls. In the distance the river
whispers, *it's time to sleep.* I wrap

my book in fern and see stars slipping
like melting ice. A fox bickers.
A rabbit pleads. I smell red wind
and shut my eyes to catch you reeling in the sun.

You left *Cill Aodáin* in a hurry – to do with
the death of a horse – odds on, a tall tale!
With hands out wide, you trudged south to Tuam,
then on to Craughwell and Gort.

You knew darkness and could measure light:
*come to me – come with me – show me your scars
and I will curse for you.*

While Saint Bridget hung washing on a sunbeam
in spring, you dreamt of being a boy again
with rod and golden worms. Flowers and lists
of red berries carpeted the bog road in *Cill Aodáin.*

There was a first night in Claremorris and
strong drink in Balla. Kiltimagh was steeped in laughter.
All this was yours for a song. A poet dreams.
A muse seeks its own geography.

You are back – a sculpture in Kiltimagh – a bard
trapped in open air for entertainment. I try to keep
an up-to-date diary of other routine events:

A woman in curlers charts a love story
in a shop window; another sings
of a long-lost lotto ticket.

Health-freaks check their feet before
walking round in circles; a footless man
peeps through the church railing.

Planes hardly clear the houses in Knock
and children are rushed off to piano lessons
and you say:
come, sit by me for a moment. I am blind.
I have walked to Galway and can hear the sun.

The child in your tomb will continue to outlive
days of holy awe and judgement –

in *Cill Aodáin* in springtime, with nature
writing colour into a new season, your silhouette,
baked in earth and sound, is stencilled in the sky.

LET'S IMAGINE
for Val and Mary Noone, Melbourne

Let's imagine barn doors never hang,
young mothers don't gather, or Raftery
never crossed *Lios Árd* in changing seasons.

He did
and his blindness
helped him
see

when a thorn bush invited him
to choose
between poetry and the fiddle.

1902 – Melbourne: in urban heat,
emigrant, Martin Hood recalls
a windfall moment in Ballylee

when he heard the bard sing of
Mary Hynes and Bridget Vasey
as if he could see them on his fingertips.

Raftery died in 1835. Let's imagine him
one hundred and seventy-five years on
reinventing himself in digital downloads,
dentists' drills and endings in DNA.

He wouldn't have learned religion, but
he'd have earth gods or alien gods.
He'd be on journeys – maybe in Facebook
and Twitter – as full of life as
the swish of a lamb's tail, or full battery.

And he'd be on something of substance and
tomfoolery in a circle of travellers
belting it out to a poached salmon lashed to a griddle.

One way or another, he is looking over a hedge
at us becoming older and children. Let's imagine.

JOURNEY OF A PEBBLE

In time and imagination
some poems
and things to do with poets
become free
like gossip in newer shape and colour,
like secret codes or
rootless tarot messages we pass on
by the day – year – century.

I kept a singing pebble from
Raftery's grave in Killeeneen
in my wallet.
It was my word, my song,
a brushstroke in the sky
and even if it never promised
to be faithful, I was sad
when it dropped into a gully
as I was walking about

near Flinder's Street Station in Melbourne.
Later I was satisfied – I had passed it on.

OPEN ROAD

With circa four thousand miles of unadopted road
in England and Wales,
poetry would appear to have a bright future.

A PORTABLE LAND

All night long a gale's been haunting our house
with me upstairs tense as a tight lip.

Gusts scream into ash, birch and thorn
like daggers at a fashion show.

The front gate and shed door jangle
and clank – shirts flap on the line.

At dawn when the moon is still, I will
step into the orange mayhem, hoping

for enough clean light by the big beech
to check passport and phantoms,

to pin my face to the page,
to prod me out to sea.

There is script upon script on streets
with strange names and habits

but whose land is this I wander?
I can live anywhere, I think,

but can I allow myself to be dictated to
by the rites of a single landscape?

At the horizon when I step over and
tuck into melting pot rations, will it

be more of the same with naked men and women
talking themselves up?

Grab that spade. Grab that book. Get the echo
of money into tune and airbrush the past.

The Tragedy

A man in hysterics crashes through the main doors
of the state theatre just as a Shakespearian tragedy
is building nicely towards a dramatic climax.

Never having been in a theatre or known the pain
of suffering on stage, he stumbles upon Hamlet
about to strangle Gertrude in her bed. *My son's*

been killed by a tram, the man pleads. Hamlet stops
beating his mother, grabs the intruder and skies him
through the wings, down into the street with the

audience in raptures. The hero adjusts his costume
and returns to his lines. Critics sing tabloids to the
director's pluck and to Hamlet's new-found resolution.

SMALL TOWNVILLE

It's strange how bookshelves, phone directories
or old photos make you think about times
that are little more than contours.

There's no doubt in my mind I'd like to have
my youth back – the youth I threw away
for a repertoire of wax candles and incense.

I'm sure I could have lived on a magic bus with
a wild woman but, instead, I oiled my bike
and polished my hair to meet choirmasters.

I sprinted up an alleyway with a shop assistant
at lunchtime. She stopped to catch her breath
by a high wall, and when no one was looking

I kissed her eyes and felt things young blood aspires to.
But when I was told of her bastard child – no one
had ever seen – I'd watch her in the shop window

from a dark place on the other side of the street.
I'd whisper her name and see her hands move
like silk. I wanted to take her to an opera; to let

our time together pass in silence. Once when
we met on the pavement, she lifted her
lavish eyes and I ducked into an open door like

I was supposed to. People knew when to smile.
A bunch of convent girls jeered from a safe distance.
I stood with lads in smoke and sweat at the church wall.

She walked past. They howled. I hid. She couldn't.
The shopkeeper and his wife thrashed her
at the church door. They'd never be late for a blessing,

and they'd no child of their own, it was said. We sang
hymns for a good while. I imagine her in a far-off land
with a photo of a boy prince spread across her brow.

LOVE DOWN THE TUBES
OR HAMLET, FOR SURE
after Kurt Tucholsky's *Blick in die Zunkunft*

In quiet moments, I think back
to the night when you whispered,
Billy ... in your demented sleep.

Was it really fever, or was I to prepare
for barstools and lonely treks on Sundays?
Billy ... there it was again, snug between your

little snorts – softer, yet unmistakeable
– *Billy*. I scrambled to my hush-hush hideout
under the doghouse floorboards
to rummage for a set of emergency battering rams.

The readiness is all.
Hamlet, I think.

I see you languishing on your *Billy* boss's knee
waist deep in fatty cakes and filthy giggles,
with me – your silent lump
hanging like a field-mouse in orbit.

I could take pleasure in those
barely audible sighs from your
Billy bed,

if you called out my name,
Gabriel,
like an anthem from a lonely hill.

The rest is silence.
Hamlet, for sure.

IN THE END …

maybe it was your picture
of a boatman on a lake

and the shadow of a child
along an autumn horizon

that made me look inwards
and not out to galaxies

where dreams are stars –
eclipses are closer to home.

I need more twilight now
to shut down on bustle, and

a place to lie down with kin
next to an open window.

CAT NAP

The black cat
on the windowsill
seems lost in
its fur management,
but I know
it has one ear on
happenings in the room
and the other on
the open window.

SMUG CAT

When you glance my way,
Cat,
you look smug and stuffy
like a cautious young thing
on a late night spree
long before midnight,

but remember
you are no longer a goddess
even if you possess
the demeanour of one
trying to recall Egyptian days
when you were worshipped,

and don't forget
your passage was controlled.
You were mummified.

Return to the ancients,
if you wish,

but bear in mind
they threw your brains
and guts to the dogs
before they stuffed you.

LIMBO

The dead were never far from us as children.
Some looked up at us from Hell, while
the shining examples were in Heaven
or nearly there after a short stop-over in Purgatory.

In our parish there were no dropouts, but there were
nameless babies in Limbo. You could see them
on nights black as tom cats or among fox cubs
in pools of dew – marked children in unmarked graves.

When I drift about in insomnia, I try to count them
but give up and return to sheep, hens or fish
because they usually have labels, tags – even names,
dates and places of burial. We are victims of gods.

Horse Dreams

The horse under the chestnut tree was not just
avoiding flies. He seemed to sleep on three legs with a
fourth resting separately. There wasn't a bloodsucker
in sight, not even a horsefly,

so I concluded he must have been dreaming when his
flank fluttered a slight shudder. Could the horse have
been reliving a blissful summer with a French pony
before castration, or

was he lost in an ancient horse song that filtered
through generations like harness, horse-sense or
breeding. Was he sad because he'd missed out on
being a rodeo star,

or a circus horse, knowing full well he didn't have the
build or looks and he'd always been uneasy in crowds.
Dream on horse. Where's my bike? It's time to return
to the song my forefathers

obliged me to continue with,
but I'll need a pouch of red wine
to get started.

IN A DOLL'S HOUSE

Day after day, year in year out, life after life,
you and I sit like puppets, or stand at the horizon
unable to trust our wings.

We make low, uneasy sounds behind frosted glass
or we toy with balloons
hoping to find a second wind.

Former lovers saunter along the street below
like links in a chain of empty cups –
like glitzy eyes dancing in tandem.

I had a full pipe and swagger then, but we grew
weary searching for each other in sweat shops,
data banks, meditation classes and crossfire.

You used to be a good kisser. I had my newspaper
in my tweed pocket. We were a repeat performance
turning left, left, left, left, left – only left.

My car was bigger than yours. You were
more brunette; better on the phone to
Indian summer resorts – things like that.

We've moved on to become decorations in an
earthenware pot – a place where
birds of prey can't stop laughing, and when you

think that, in our day, The Beatles sang
love, love, love,
love is all you need … love is all you need.

In a doll's house next door, a healthy boy
is getting singing lessons
to make him more tenor, to make him more base,

to suppress his love
of singing songs,
to make him one of us.

THE ONLY LEGEND I HAVE EVER LOVED

When she spun round my front door
in her fiery hatchback,
hares teamed up with dogs,
insects took to the hills breathless.
My bike was rattled but stayed put.

What do you work at?
was her first question
after ten minutes of dating
in a flashy place I couldn't afford.

Teacher, I'm a teacher.
Ah well.

I was Socrates on trial, staring
at my ladder sinking
into terrible destiny in a cell.

Silent as a blouse, she stared
into her glass saying she enjoyed
being private with a man.

Baffled in silence and tongue-tied,
I looked to the crescent moon for help
before cocktail and cloud took over.

Even Socrates must have shifted from
foot to foot before finally drinking.
Always ask a hero first, I'd read somewhere.

Anyway, we jumped ahead into what felt like
another skin
until one evening my new partner sang:

and if we don't buy that pram soon, we'll
have to consider importing from China
so under a full moon, we lashed up
the *Autobahn* to IKEA,
and belted back with colour camera

and pram in digital
before mothers-in-laws or Chinese
got wind of our intention.

The only legend I have ever loved
is the tale of a woman and a teacher,
and the good thing is
it's only beginning and I am learning.

LOVE

He a juggler on unicycle bike –
she a dancer on thinnest of ice
– her breakthrough came.

He packed up juggling – she dancing.
He took up skating – she clowning –
they needed to be certain of their love.

Ducks quack, lay eggs and swim.
The drake pops up now and then.
It's easier.

A Perfect Family in Arles

We, hand in hand in France –waiting for coffee
in sunny Arles – when the perfect family of four
occupied all twenty-nine seats on our side of the street.

The mother tall, large and he every bit the basher in
club yellow – their daughters, dark, leggy in pink
screaming: *we've had enough of culture and vulture!*

Dad took pride of place, raised a racket and informed
his offspring he was doing churches and museums
because he adored them, worshiped Mum and he was

footing the bills. The leggy girls in pink hid behind
their knees while he chanted: *You will serve me as
I have served you with forehands and backhands in*

times of need. We are a pious people, a chosen people. Our
table upped and left like a soul with a place to go to.
We meandered off down the cobblestones into the wings.

The chanting went on and on. Streets emptied. Chairs
deserted their place at table. Dogs left bones where
they were. The man stripped, began pumping iron,
ripped his loved ones

of things, moaned, groaned, while daughters sang a
hymn to a homeland of family values and club
something uniforms. His wife ate furiously, silently
enunciating his words. Later,

in another part of town, we watched them studying a
mighty cathedral door. We wondered what to do –
wondered about going to a bullfight – groups were
gathering on street corners.

AT A SHOP DOOR IN SLOUGH
for Matthew

Oh, I am so sorry, thought you was a lady!

A woman was holding a door open for me
with Matthew asleep in his pushchair.

*You see, it's usually the lady what pushes
the chair. I expected you to be a mum.*

Thanks, anyway.

*Awfully sorry, but it's usually a lady,
isn't it? I wasn't looking. Happy New Year.*

To you too, and thanks for holding the door for us.

The woman rushed away, looking back,
lilting *sorry, terribly sorry* to every step.

*The wheels on the bus go round and round,
round and round, round and round.*

*The wheels on the bus go round and round,
all day long.*

There's nothing to beat a man
that's only half a man and half a woman
and they pushing a pram.

GROUNDS FOR BURIAL
a poem in eight parts …

I

SO MUCH DEPENDS ON DEATH

The cat and fox are true cynics.
They have the rabbit pinned down.

This time, we'll finish him, but
we have no intention of sharing him,

they seem to say, as they sit like misfits
on either side of the rabbit burrow.

Neither cat nor fox give an inch
for an hour. Then perfect and unbeaten,

they strut in opposite directions like
a couple of be-and-end-alls. Intrusion:

a politician is using the radio to appeal
to good nature. Cat and fox beware.

He is the sniper you cannot see in the flatness
he has created. So much depends on death.

II

AN ABRUPT END

I'm reading a really good story about
a woman called *Opfer* who takes us

through the process of hanging herself.
She is high up on a branch, wind-tossed,

with her head in a noose – she has eyes
for her man, only, and he's below

in her best rival's garden as exposed
as a chocolate biscuit in sun.

The story finishes abruptly – her
final plea wasted on the wind – like

a child calling out from under bedclothes
– and just as it was getting good.

III

SOLEMN SILENCE

A monk is king in a cell full of books
– his trash out of sight to everyone,

except bees buzzing home to his hives
after a long day in nectar fields.

Who knows what folds of secrets
his solemn silence holds.

His lips move. His sounds are hidden.
He'd be mad to kill himself. No story.

IV

WEIRDO

But what about Weirdo who survived cutting his throat?
It is said he'd stand at the bar like a prince – he'd walk

up and down, up and down, up down
with a hand on his throat and his head to one side

to cover up … and he could be daft – *boy, could he
tell them!* He didn't smile at others, but to himself

and he kept moving up and down along the bar
over and back. Nobody minded – he was good *craic*.

His would be a good story – it has never been told
and nobody cares, but a writer could make it up:

fill in the blanks, the tears; goodbye note to his mother,
even take photos – called images. The poet could sit

at the end of the bar – left alone to capture a script
called 'The Man With the Scar' – a working title.

Weirdo's granny would be a queen among whores,
his mother an invalid in bottles and fantasy literature.

The book would be borne aloft along High Street.
There'd be bikes against walls and twenty hands

attached to every mobile at the publisher's. Weirdo
was a header – he could be heard down by the river.

V

WHOSE LIFE WAS IT!

The years before his birth were his best years.
He was still a dream, a desire – a kicking object

a second hand – a man about the house. His father
had sometimes laughed for he'd been heard

beyond the boundaries of his daily drudge.
They had a party after his birth. He was a boy.

They called him Paddy – Paddy Maguire and
quickly harnessed him to a plough in case

he thought to get beyond his station.
He might have dreamt of women, especially

after a day among wet ridges and drills.
When his parents died, he was captured

by the poet, Kavanagh,
and trapped between his lines:

for all to sneer at,
for all to pity,

for all to scoff at as he faced into a fence
when desire became urgent.

VI

UNTITLED

What has Paddy got to do with Weirdo?
Not much. You could take their story anywhere.

They'd share the same jackdaws, rain,
blackbirds, turf-barrows, force of silence and

for the sake of obedience and fear,
they'd go to Sunday mass to say *sorry*.

What has Paddy got to do with *Opfer*?
Nothing except, had they met they'd

probably have got tackled to the same plough,
and been shovelled over with wet mud

or they might have escaped into a kingdom
where syllables were obsolete and the light

from the black moon gave off enough light
for the last chapter of their journey.

Enough about all that – let's move on.

VII

DEATH MY COMEDY

It is said
death doesn't read

death doesn't dream
death doesn't do.

What does death do apart from
dying and rotting?

What if a woman spent her life
admiring herself in a pond

like a female Narcissus, and
what if her ashes were thrown

into that very same water – would
ashes turn to self for solace

instead of becoming shades
of watercolour, or would the

rejuvenated ashes turn
to a sacred book to reincarnate?

There are signs of mortality everywhere:
out in the fields, among the hedgerows;

in an ageing handshake; in facelifts or
in a reader who slowly gives up reading.

My father was my age once. I am
more than the combined ages of my sons.

I line up to take my place in
The Divine Comedy ... what matter!

Hell, Purgatory, Heaven.
Father, Son and Holy Spirit,

bunches of three – early mornings
late afternoons and evenings,

fragments, driftwood, dislocated dreams.
Take another look at a poet in panic

and ask yourself if he's trying to keep
his soul from escaping. Fragments,

driftwood, dislocated dreams that wilt
the moment the scribe is distracted

or turns his back for a moment to die.
What did the poet look like? What colour

was the hair on his scull where holes
have replaced lost eyes, mouths and nostrils.

A bone is a bone.
A peddler on wheels is a pedlar.

VIII

Ones Like Me

I lay asleep in a far-off land dreaming I was
a puppet prince facing death, but I didn't die.

Instead I closed my window, shook myself
and turned to the first pen and page I could dig up.

Now read on:

I left home, a small, four-footed virgin
out of place and quiet as a bar of chocolate.

In my first room I had a bed, a pair of lamps,
a bicycle, a book and an open window to let

the hard music of a header invade my life.
Two stinky feet are bad, but with four

you get dirty looks in the bank
and no insurance company will touch you.

Phase two began at eighteen when I saw
a dark woman, who wasn't my mother,

on the far side of the railway tracks. Doctors
sidled past eying me for traces of mortality.

A man wearing a half-open cassock came by.
We skinned a rabbit. He drank enough, too.

I should have killed him but, as he was not
a she, I didn't submit, or look at his photos.

I might have got caught up in the slave trade,
have been locked up in a classroom with

several women at a time – with no faith
beyond wishful thinking and opening chapters.

Phase three. Answer any three questions:
a) What is sex?
b) What is sex?
c) What is sex?

I raced up two, three, thirty-nine steps
with a blonde and me on question three.

At the same time, I was tuned into
the death forecast for years to come

with the remains of my chocolate coating
melting in the heat of blue movies,

electric fires, city girls and hi-tech wires.
I had myself cross-examined:

there was no shortage of nonsense
in my head

in my heart
in my gut

in the park
in a house full of newly-weds.

Complete the following multiple-choice question:

A) nicotine heals heartbreak
B) nicotine heals heartthrob

C) nicotine heals heart-attack
D) nicotine heals heart-arrest

Which is correct?
A only B only C only D only,
ABC or D
Neither ABC nor D.

Therapy time. As a kid in primary school,
I didn't have four feet, but when I got

a father and mother of a hammering
for having two left ones in front of the goal,

I soon realized I'd need four for a while, as
my father, his wife and their family loved football.

They howled, clapped, yahooed, whistled,
swore, cursed, goaded, guffawed and

cheered everyone wildly, but me.
In the river, four feet were better than three,

and they were a godsend when I had to
pull a dogcart or do donkey-work delivering

prime cuts and guts to cherubs. Conclusion:
ones like me will always be

as long as four foot two remains four foot two.
I have enough material to begin my book.

The light is better and
the burial ground is over there among my people.

Terry McDonagh is from County Mayo and lives in the West of Ireland and in Germany. His poetry collections include *The Road Out*, *A World Without Stone*, *A Song for Joanna*, *Boxes*, *Cill Aodáin and Nowhere Else* illustrated by Sally McKenna (Blaupause-Books, Hamburg), *The Truth in Mustard* (Arlen House) and *In the Light of Bridges: Hamburg Fragments* (Blaupause-Books, Hamburg). He edited *Through That Door* for Clare County Library in 2009. His poetry has been translated into German and Indonesian. He is currently completing a bilingual English/German illustrated story set in Hamburg, entitled *Michel the Merman*.

Terry has taught English at Hamburg University and was Drama Director at The International School, Hamburg. His other work includes drama, *I Wanted to Bring You Flowers* (Fischer, Aachen); fiction, *One Summer in Ireland* (Klett, Stuttgart); letters, *Elbe Letters Go West* (Blaupause) and *Twelve Strange Songs*, poems put to music for voice and string quartet by the late Eberhard Reichel, Hamburg.